SUPER SANDCASTLE·
Poetry Power

CARROTS
~TO~
CUPCAKES

Reading, Writing, and Reciting
Poems About Food

COMPILED & EDITED BY SUSAN M. FREESE   ILLUSTRATED BY JAN WESTBERG

ABDO
Publishing Company

Published by ABDO Publishing Company, 8000 West 78th Street, Edina, MN 55439. Copyright © 2008 by Abdo Consulting Group, Inc. International copyrights reserved in all countries. No part of this book may be reproduced in any form without written permission from the publisher. Super SandCastle™ is a trademark and logo of ABDO Publishing Company.

Printed in the United States.

Editor: Pam Price
Curriculum Coordinator: Nancy Tuminelly
Cover and Interior Design and Production: Mighty Media

Library of Congress Cataloging-in-Publication Data

Freese, Susan M., 1958-
  Carrots to cupcakes : reading, writing, and reciting poems about food /
  Susan M. Freese.
    p. cm. -- (Poetry power)
  Includes index.
  ISBN 978-1-60453-003-2
1. Poetry--Authorship--Juvenile literature. 2. Children's poetry, American.
3. Food in literature--Juvenile literature. I. Title.

PN1059.A9 F743
808.1--dc22

2007037590

Super SandCastle™ books are created by a team of professional educators, reading specialists, and content developers around five essential components— phonemic awareness, phonics, vocabulary, text comprehension, and fluency— to assist young readers as they develop reading skills and strategies and increase their general knowledge. All books are written, reviewed, and leveled for guided reading, early intervention reading, and Accelerated Reader® programs for use in shared, guided, and independent reading and writing activities to support a balanced approach to literacy instruction.

About SUPER SANDCASTLE™

Bigger Books for Emerging Readers Grades PreK–3

Created for library, classroom, and at-home use, Super SandCastle™ books support and engage young readers as they develop and build literacy skills and will increase their general knowledge about the world around them. Super SandCastle™ books are part of SandCastle™, the leading preK–3 imprint for emerging and beginning readers. Super SandCastle™ features a larger trim size for more reading fun.

Let Us Know

Super SandCastle™ would like to hear your stories about reading this book. What was your favorite page? Was there something hard that you needed help with? Share the ups and downs of learning to read. We want to hear from you! Send us an e-mail.
sandcastle@abdopublishing.com

Contact us for a complete list of SandCastle™, Super SandCastle™, and other nonfiction and fiction titles from ABDO Publishing Company.
www.abdopublishing.com
8000 West 78th Street Edina, MN 55439
800-800-1312 · 952-831-1632 fax

A Note to Librarians, Teachers, and Parents

The poems in this book are grouped into three sections. "I Can Read" has poems that children can read on their own. "Read With Me" has poems that may require some reading help. "Kids' Corner" has poems written by children.

There are some words in these poems that young readers may not know. Some of these words are in boldface. Their pronunciations and definitions are given in the text. Other words can be looked up in the book's glossary.

When possible, children should first read each poem out loud. That way they will hear all of the sounds and feel all of the rhythms. If it is not possible to read aloud, instruct them to read the poems to themselves so they hear the words in their heads.

The **Poetry Pal** next to each poem explains how the poet uses words and specific styles or techniques to make the reader feel or know something.

The **Speak Up!** sidebar prompts readers to reflect on what they think each poem means and how it relates to them.

Become a Poet! provides ideas and activities to encourage and enhance learning about reading, writing, and reciting poetry.

Contents

What Is

Let's pretend someone has asked you to write about your favorite food. Maybe that is ice cream or pizza. But you have to follow these rules for writing. First, you can't use very many words. And second, you have to put the words in order so they make a rhyme or a rhythm when you read them.

These are some of the rules for writing poetry. Poetry is different from the writing you do at school and other places, which is called **prose** (PROZE). Here's how!

Poets, the people who write poetry, use fewer words than other kinds of writers. That means they have to pick just the right words to say what they think and feel. The words in poems often are about how things look, feel, smell, taste, and sound. Poets use words to paint pictures for their readers.

4

poetry?

Poets also arrange words in ways to create rhyme and rhythm. You probably know that words that **rhyme** (RIME) sound the same, such as *cat*, *sat*, and *bat*. Rhyming words are fun to say and to hear. A **rhythm** (RIH-thum) is a pattern of sounds. Think about the beat you feel when you clap or march to music. You can feel the same kind of beat when you read a poem. By using rhythm and rhyme, poets make words sound like music.

What else is special about poetry? Because of all the choices poets get to make when they write, no two poems are ever the same. You will see that when you read the poems in this book! And you will find that out when you write your own poems too!

C
S at
B

Getting Started

The terms on the next page are about how poets choose words and put them together in special ways. As you read about each term, look at the poem "Meal Deals" to see an example.

Meal Deals

BY SAM FOWLER

At my house, at every meal,
Mom and I must make a deal.
For each food I hate to eat,
She must find a special treat.

Salad earns a donut hole.
Ice cream follows casserole.
Broccoli brings a chocolate shake.
Liver means a big cupcake!

line

A line in a poem is a group of words written across the page. In "Meal Deals," the first line is "At my house, at every meal." Each new line starts below the one before it. There are eight lines in this short poem.

stanza
(STAN-zuh)

A stanza is a group of lines in a poem that are usually about the same idea. A stanza is like a paragraph in other kinds of writing. Stanzas are separated by blank lines of space. "Meal Deals" has two stanzas.

rhyme
(RIME)

Words that rhyme end with the same sound, such as *dog* and *log* and *fox* and *socks*. In a poem, the last words of the lines often rhyme but not always. In many poems, every pair of lines rhymes or every other line rhymes. In "Meal Deals," every pair of lines rhymes. For example, lines 1 and 2 end with *meal* and *deal*. And lines 3 and 4 end with *eat* and *treat*.

rhythm
(RIH-thum)

Even poems that don't rhyme have rhythm, a pattern of sounds or beats. In most poems, some sounds are accented. That means you say them with a little more punch. Read "Meal Deals" aloud and listen to which sounds you accent. Clap on these sounds to help you hear and feel them. You probably read line 1 using a pattern like this, "**AT** my **HOUSE** at **EV**-ery **MEAL**." To read this line, you accent every other sound, starting with the first one. Line 2 has the same pattern, and so do the rest of the lines. All the lines in this poem have the same rhythm.

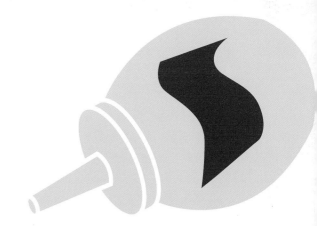

I Can Read

8

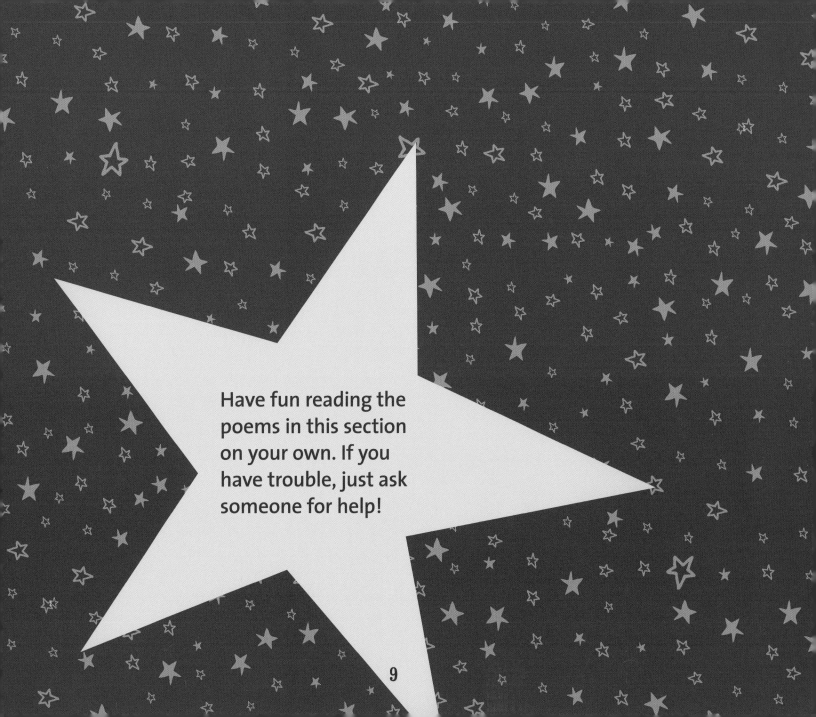

Have fun reading the poems in this section on your own. If you have trouble, just ask someone for help!

9

Recipe

BY JOYCE ARMOR

First you take a giant bowl
and put a waffle in it,
then you add a bunch of jam
and stir it for a minute.

After that you get a cup
and fill it up with custard,
then dump it in with mushroom soup
and just a little mustard.

Squeeze a lemon right on top,
add peanut butter—oodles,
but don't forget the applesauce
and two big scoops of noodles.

Then nuke it in the microwave,
That's it, you've got a winner.
Get the plates out now and yell,
"Come and get it! Dinner!"

Things to Do If You Are a Pizza

by Bobbi Katz

Get started by a man who wears a white hat.
Get stretched and pulled and thrown in the air.
Get shaped in a circle,
Sprinkled with cheese,
Slurped with sauce,
Slipped in an oven.
Sizzle.
Bubble.
Watch out! Someone will eat you!

POETRY PAL

The title tells you that this poem is going to be silly. It's a list of things for a pizza to do! In a poem, a list like this is called a **catalog** (CAT-uh-log).

If you read the list again, you'll see that it gives the steps for making a pizza. This poem is really a recipe!

SPEAK UP!

This poem has a lot of words that are fun to say, such as *slurped* and *sizzle* and *bubble*. Write down three fun words that tell about your favorite food.

The Proper Way to Eat

BY JOHN FRANK

The way to eat your lunch meat
is to roll it into tubes.
The way to eat your Jell-O
is to jiggle all the cubes.
The way to eat your Swiss cheese
is to nibble it like mice.
The way to eat your water
is to chew the chunks of ice.
The way to eat your doughnut
is to try to save the hole.
The way to eat your ice cream
is to overfill the bowl.

The way to eat your pudding
is to suck it through a straw.
The way to eat your peanuts
is to store them in your jaw.
The way to eat your apple
is to munch it like a hog.
The way to eat your spinach
is to feed it to your dog.
The way to eat your noodles
is in one unending slurp.
The way to end your meal
is with a record-breaking BURP.

SPEAK UP!

Think of some food that
you eat in a special way.
Then write a new line in your
poetry journal for the poem by
filling in the blanks. The way to
eat your _____ is to _____.

13

POETRY PAL

Did you ever think that vegetables could be so much fun? You've probably never seen them come to life!

Talking about things like they're people is called **personification** (purr-sahn-iff-ih-KAY-shun). Poets use personification to make things seem alive and real. List all the things in the poem that make the vegetables seem like people.

SPEAK UP!

Imagine another vegetable that could join the Veggie Soup band. What instrument would it play? Draw the new veggie character playing its instrument in your poetry journal.

Veggie Soup

BY JIM AYLESWORTH

Carl Carrot is lead singer
In a band called Veggie Soup.
They're old-time country/western,
And they're quite a well-known group.

Bo Beet, he plays the fiddle.
He's the best, folks say, by far.
Oz Onion, he's on banjo,
And Tex Tater plays guitar.

They all wear fringe and rhinestones,
Fancy hats and cowboy boots,
And everybody loves 'em,
From young kids to real old coots.

You Can't Make Me Eat That

BY JACK PRELUTSKY

You can't make me eat that,
it's slimy and gooey
and icky and yucky
and greasy and gluey.
It looks like you made it
from maggots and mud,
some chopped hippopotamus,
bug heads and blood.

I hate it, I hate it,
I hate it to bits!
Just thinking about it
is giving me fits.
One taste and I'm certain
I'll instantly die…
You can't make me eat that,
so don't even try.

POETRY PAL

Read this poem aloud to hear the fun sounds of the words! In lines 2, 3, and 4, find all the words that end with an *e* sound, such as *slimy*. In lines 5 and 6, look for words with *el* and *em* sounds. What sounds are repeated in lines 7 and 8?

Patterns of sounds in poems are called **sound devices**.

SPEAK UP!

What food won't you eat, no matter what? Why?

15

Read With Me

Enjoy reading these
poems with someone
who can help you with
the harder words and
ideas. Poetry is more fun
when you understand
what you are reading!

17

Food Fight

BY KENN NESBITT

We'd never seen the teachers
in a state of such distress.
The principal was yelling
that the lunchroom was a mess.

It started off so innocent
when someone threw a bun,
but all the other kids decided
they should join the fun.

It instantly turned into
an enormous lunchroom feud,
as students started hurling
all their halfway-eaten food.

18

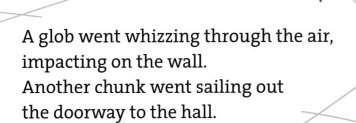

A glob went whizzing through the air,
impacting on the wall.
Another chunk went sailing out
the doorway to the hall.

The food was splattered everywhere—
the ceilings, walls, and doors.
A sloppy, gloppy mess was on
the tables and the floors.

And so our good custodian
ran out to grab his mop.
It took him half the afternoon
to clean up all the slop.

The teachers even used some words
we're not supposed to mention.
And that's how all the kids and teachers
wound up in detention.

19

SPEAK UP!

Words such as *hurling* and *splattered* help readers see the food fight in their minds. Which part of the food fight do you see most clearly? Pick your favorite stanza.

A Tasty Conversation for Two Voices

BY BOBBI KATZ

Said peanut butter to the jelly,
"Slide across my nice tan belly."

Jelly answers all a flutter,
"Here I am, dear peanut butter!"

Two friends, true friends,
we taste yummy
on our way to someone's tummy.

Two friends, true friends,
we taste yummy
on our way to someone's tummy.

20

Big Lunch

BY KENN NESBITT

I started arranging my alphabet soup,
concocting big words to devour.
I swallowed a BUILDING.
I gobbled a STREET,
and then I ingested a TOWER.

I snacked on a SUBWAY.
I bolted a BUS.
I wolfed down a PASSENGER TRAIN.
I chewed up MONTANA.
I gulped INDIANA,
then tossed down the whole STATE OF MAINE.

I ate the GRAND CANYON.
I lunched on the ROCKIES,
and ASIA, I slurped from my cup.
I would have been fine,
but I started to dine
on MY HOMEWORK,
and then I threw up.

21

POETRY PAL

The **speaker**, the person talking in this poem, is having a really big lunch! Count all the lines that begin like *I swallowed* and *I gobbled*.

Words such as *swallowed* and *gobbled* are **verbs**. They tell about actions or doing things. In this poem, the verbs are about eating!

SPEAK UP!

The title of this poem makes a little joke! Think of two ways that the speaker has a big lunch. One way is by eating too much. What is the other way?

What would you say to get out of eating food you hate? The speaker in this poem tries all kinds of things. In stanza 1, the speaker says "no thanks, not today." In stanza 2, the speaker talks about maybe begging for liver tomorrow. What does the speaker say in stanza 3? Here's where the truth comes out!

The speaker goes on and on about hating liver, even making up a few things. Stretching the truth like this is called **hyperbole** (hy-PURR-bow-lee).

Sliver of Liver

BY LOIS SIMMIE

Just a sliver of liver they want me to eat,
It's good for my blood, they all say;
They want me to eat just the tiniest sliver
Of yukky old slimy old slithery liver;
I'm saying no thanks, not today.

No, I'll pass for tonight but tomorrow I might
Simply beg for a sliver of liver.
"Give me liver!" I'll cry. "I'll have liver or die!
Oh, please cook me a sliver of liver!"
One piece might not do, I'll need two or a few,
I'll want tons of the wobbly stuff,
Of that quivery shivery livery pile
There may not be nearly enough.

Just a sliver, you say? No thanks, not today.
Tomorrow, I really can't say;
But today I would sooner eat slivers of glass,
Eat the tail of a skunk washed down with gas,
Eat slivers of sidewalks and slivers of swings,
Slivers and slivers of any old thing,
Than a sliver of slimy old quivery shivery
Livery liver today.

SPEAK UP!

Now it's your turn to stretch the truth. What would you rather eat than your most-hated food? Write down two silly or awful things that you'd offer to eat. Just pretending, of course.

Eggs!

BY JACK PRELUTSKY

Eggs!
You're excellent, exquisite,
I exalt you, hot or cold,
I salute you in a salad,
I commend you in a mold,
you are scrumptious lightly scrambled,
fully fascinating fried,
incandescent over easy,
dazzling on your sunny side.

Eggs!
You're dainty when you're coddled,
when you're stuffed, I long to bite,
you're angelic when you're deviled,
when you're shirred, you're sheer delight,
you are magic on a muffin,
gold ambrosia on a bun,
you are princely, poached precisely,
when your yellow starts to run.

Eggs!
You're nectar in an omelette,
in soufflés, a savory dream,
baked or boiled you are bewitching,
in a quiche, you reign supreme,
yes, I love you to distraction,
but alas, you have a flaw,
for you're thoroughly revolting
when you're swallowed whole and raw.

SPEAK UP!

The last three lines of the poem tell what the speaker hates about eggs! Think about your favorite food. What do you like most about it? What do you hate about it?

25

A poem that looks like what it's about is called a **concrete** (kahn-KREET) **poem.**

One way to write a concrete poem is to put the words inside a shape. First write down the words in lines or sentences. Then draw a picture of what your poem is about. Leave enough open space where the words will go. After you finish the picture, write the words in the open space.

Hot Dog

BY TOUA VUE

A hot dog is thin and long
When you eat it you get strong

When a hot dog is cooked hot
You will want to eat a lot

When you see my long hot dog
It will remind you of a log

Cookies

BY SARAH FULLER

Chocolate chip

Oatmeal

Oreo

Keebler

Iced

Easter

Shortbread

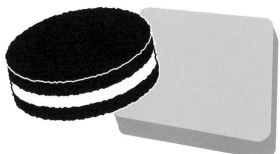

27

Become a Poet!

Here are some activities to help you write your own poems.

Keep a Journal

Many writers keep a journal, which is a book of ideas, thoughts, and drawings. Start your own journal in an empty notebook. Write down ideas for your own poems. Write down things that happen, what you like and don't like. Keep your journal with you so you can use it often.

Learn New Words

In the back of your journal, make a list of new words you learn. Start with the words you learned while reading the poems in this book. Write down each word and what it means. Then write each word in a sentence to make sure you know how to use it. Also write down how to say it if you think you won't remember.

Make a Picture

Draw or paint a picture about one of the poems in this book. Maybe pick one of the poems that has many words about colors and other things you can see. Share both the poem and the picture with someone.

Write a Story

Choose one of the poems in this book and write a story from it. Your story can be about what's happening in the poem or who's in the poem. Write using your own words, not the words from the poem.

Have a Poetry Reading

With a few friends or family members, put on a show where everyone has a turn to read a poem out loud. When people aren't reading, they should be in the audience. Practice using correct rhythm and rhyme beforehand. Also make sure you know all the words. Try reciting the poem from memory, if you can.

Find More Poems

What's your favorite poem in this book? Who wrote it? Use the Internet and books in your library to find another poem by this poet. Read the new poem several times. Then read your favorite poem again. How are the two poems alike? How are they different? Which poem do you like best now? Write about the poems in your journal.

Learn About Poets

Use the Internet or books in your library to learn about famous poets. Start with Bobbi Katz, who writes a lot of children's poems. Where is she from? What poems has she written? Read four poems by Bobbi Katz and pick your favorite. Write down in your journal why you like this poem the best.

Make a Recording

Record yourself reading one of the poems from this book out loud. Practice so you can read the poem with the correct rhythm and rhyme. Ask your parent or teacher for help, if you need it. Record other poems later to make a set of your favorite poems.

Glossary

commend – to praise.

concoct – to create or make.

coot – an odd but harmless person.

detention – a punishment where a student is made to remain at school after hours.

distress – pain or suffering in the mind or body.

exalt – to honor.

exquisite – perfect and beautiful.

fascinating – very interesting or charming.

feud – a long-lasting fight or disagreement.

impact – to hit something with force.

incandescent – glowing or shining.

ingest – to swallow.

innocent – not meaning to cause harm.

precisely – exactly.

rhinestone – a fake jewel.

savory – tasty.

scrumptious – delightful and delicious.

Permissions

Index